Daily Spelling Journal

SPELL @ NOW

This daily spelling journal

belongs to

_____

Curriculum Concepts
comprehensive coverage

Spell Now – Book 4
ISBN 9781906125691
Ordering Code – UK6204

Curriculum Concepts UK
The Old School
Upper High Street
Bedlinog
Mid-Glamorgan CF46 6SA
Email: orders@curriculumconcepts.co.uk
www.curriculumconcepts.co.uk

Published in United Kingdom, 2007
Copyright © Curriculum Concepts, NZ

Testing Record

List

bath
done
cry
end
first
church
soon
paper

Extension

bathroom
undo undone
cries crying cried

Interest Words

▶ Match the word with the picture:

first

church

bath

cry

2 Put 'ir', 'er', 'ur', 'or' in the blanks.

h_ _   und _ _   ch_ _ ch

d_ _ty   ov_ _   togeth_ _

f_ _ st   w_ _ k   h_ _ t

t_ _ n   fath_ _   sh_ _ t

pap_ _   c_ _ l   b_ _ d

3 Find the hidden words:

firstuvcryzabendefgchurchibathijkldonefgsoonm

Write them here:

_____   _____   _____

_____   _____   _____

_____   **Which** list word
                 is missing?   _____

4 ▶ Sometimes 'y' says 'ee' at the end of a word and sometimes it says 'i'.

• Write these words in the right columns:

> teddy   my   fly   cry   why   try
> by   very   only   carry   any

'y' says 'i'	'y' says 'ee'

5 ▶ Write a list or extension word to fill in each gap:

"Don't _____ please Kim", begged Mum.

"We can go home _____ before church and

give you a_____."

"But Mum, look what I've _____ ! I've spilt

egg all down myself and my dress," cried Kim.

"Here's the _____ of our street. We'll be home

very _____." said Mum.

Testing Record

List	Extension
camp	camping camper
hold	held
shell	shellfish
high	
bend	
pick	
club	
change	

Interest Words

▶ Match the words with the same blends:

ki**nd**	change
lu**mp**	club
child	hold
bui**ld**	shell
ship	camp
c**l**ean	bend

2 Unjumble these 'ck' words:

clakb   _ _ _ _ _

kbac   _ _ _ _

udkc   _ _ _ _

pcki   _ _ _ _

3 Write list words in these sentences:

• I will _____ the _____ I found at _____ .

• _____ over and _____ up that _____ .

• We can go to the _____ rooms after school.

• Can you _____ the lightbulb for me? It is

too _____ .

4 **Complete** these word trees with list words:

Testing Record

List	Extension
last	lastly lasting
neck	necklace
rise	rose
spend	spent
both	
drug	
tea	
leave	

Interest Words

▶ **What** is the word?

To go up is to _____ .

You and I = _____ of us.

Opposite of first. _____

This is between our shoulders and our head. _____

We can drink or eat this. _____

Another name for medicine. _____

2 **Which** list words have a long 'e' sound?

_____

- *Write* some other '**ea**' words:

_ _ t   r_ _ d   _____

pl _ _ se   cl _ _ n   _____

3 A **homonym** is a word that sounds the same as another but is spelt differently and has a different meaning:

- *Write* the homonym for tea:

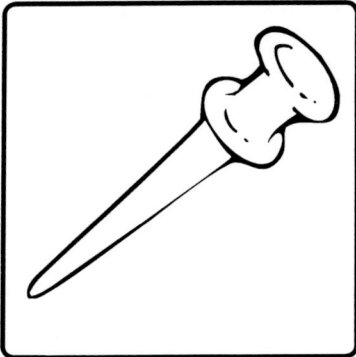

_ ee

What game do I play when I use a tee?   g _____ .

4 ▶

<u>Rise</u> is the <u>present</u> tense,

<u>rose</u> is the <u>past</u> tense.

Past, present and future tenses tell us about yesterday, today and tomorrow:

• **Choose** the correct word for the gaps.

The sun will (rise, rose) _____ tomorrow.

The sun (rise, rose) _____ yesterday.

5 ▶ **Which** list or extension words can you find and **Unjumble**?

psnte

irse

nekc

tae

stlyal

thob

sepnd

slta

veale

urgd

• *Write* them here:

_____

_____

_____

_____

Testing Record

List

place
train
stick
send
socks
drum
stamp
such

Extension

trainer

stuck stack stock

drummer

Interest Words

When we *write* a list of nouns we use **commas**.
A comma looks like this - **,** or **,**

• *Write* the nouns from the list with commas in between:

p_ _ _ _, st_ _ _   _ _ _ _s

_ r _ _   _ _ _ i _   _ _ _ m _.

A comma is a punctuation mark. It tells us to pause when we're reading or writing sentences or items in a list or between numbers.

2 Write the words in the correct shapes:

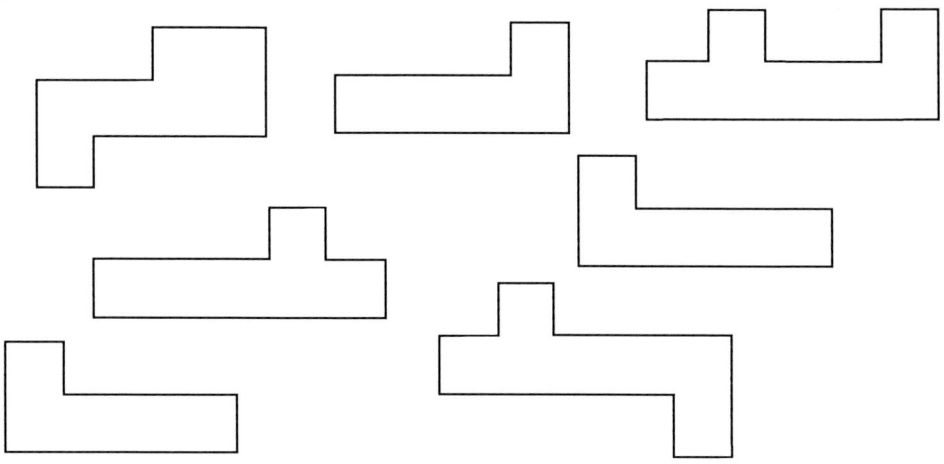

. . . .

3 **Answer** these questions with sentences:

(Q) **What do you wear on your feet inside your shoes?**

(A) **I wear _____ on my feet inside my shoes.**

(Q) **What travels on railway lines?**

(A) **A _____ travels on _____ _____ .**

(Q) **How do we send letters?**

(A) **We _____ _____ through the post.**

(Q) **What type of instrument is a drum?**

(A) **A _____ is a percussion _____ .**

4 ▶ Write the vowels:

____ ____ ____ ____ ____

• Write the list words in the column if they have that vowel in them:

a	e	i	o	u

• Circle the words with a short vowel sound.

• **Which** word is in two lists?

_____

> • **What** vowel sound does it have? _____

• Write other words with the 'ai' sound:

b _ _ t   m _ _ n   ag _ _ n

p _ _ n   r _ _ n   w _ _ t

• **How** do you remember to spell words like this? **Talk** to a friend.

_____

_____

Testing Record

List	Extension
sack	sick sock suck
step	
cheese	
tin	
began	begin
dug	
start	started starter
swam	swimming swim

Interest Words

▶ *Join* the words that are similar; they are called synonyms.

bag   tin

pace   start

can   sack

begin   step

2 If a verb has a short vowel sound, we double the last consonant before adding a suffix:

step	step+p+ing	= stepping
step	step+p+ed	= _____
tin	tin+n+ed	= _____
drum	drum+m+er	= _____
swim	swim+m+ing	= _____
hug	hug+g+ing	= _____
hop	hop+p+ed	= _____
dig	dig+g+ing	= _____

3 **Which** list word is a food made from milk?

_____

• *Write* some more food words:

‒ ‒ ‒

‒ ‒ ‒ ‒

•**Choose** the right words:

We (ate, eat) _____ (food, fill) _____

with our (tooth, teeth).

Which list words are "past tense" words?

_____   _____   _____

• *Write* the present tenses of each word.

_____   _____   _____

•**Complete** these sentences. Write your own sentences for the other words.

We will _____ a big hole.

The hole they _____ was very big.

They are _____ a hole for a tree.

5 A star point may give you a beginning or an ending.
Use '**st**' to make the words:

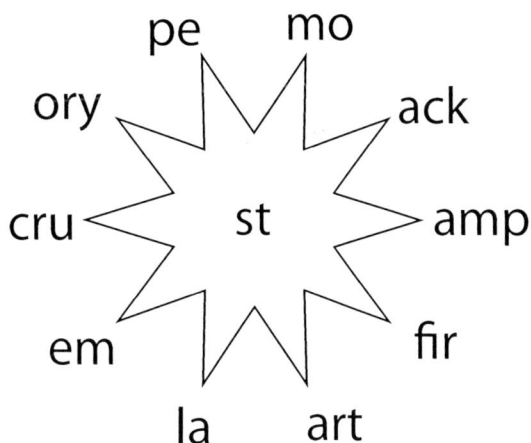

st_____   _____st

st_____   _____st

st_____   _____st

st_____   _____st

st_____   _____st

pe   mo
ory   ack
cru   st   amp
em   fir
la   art

Testing Record

List	Extension
walk	walkway
cloud	cloudy cloudless
dump	damp
stop	stopping stopped stops
tiny	tiniest
yell	
near	
balloon	

Interest Words

▶ *Write* the small words inside these words:

tiny   **near**   **stop**

cloud   **balloon**

· **What** can you add to these words?

near + ____ = _____   cloud + ____ = _____

2 Antonyms are opposites. *Write* the list words that are the antonyms of these words:

go _____

run _____

huge _____

whisper _____

· ·

3 *Write* the list words in alphabetical order:

· ·

4 **Change** walk to yell in *four* steps: *Write* a rhyme for each word:

walk _____

wal_

w_l_

yell _____

5 Complete the following:

• **Which** list words are these phrases mnemonics for?

> Mnemonics are an idea or process (usually letters) you invent to help jog your memory, to help you remember something.

Dogs use more pens._____

You eat little lollies.   _____

• **Make** up your own mnemonic for walk and near:

w_____ a_____ l_____ k_____

h_____ e_____ a_____ r_____

6 Complete the word puzzle:

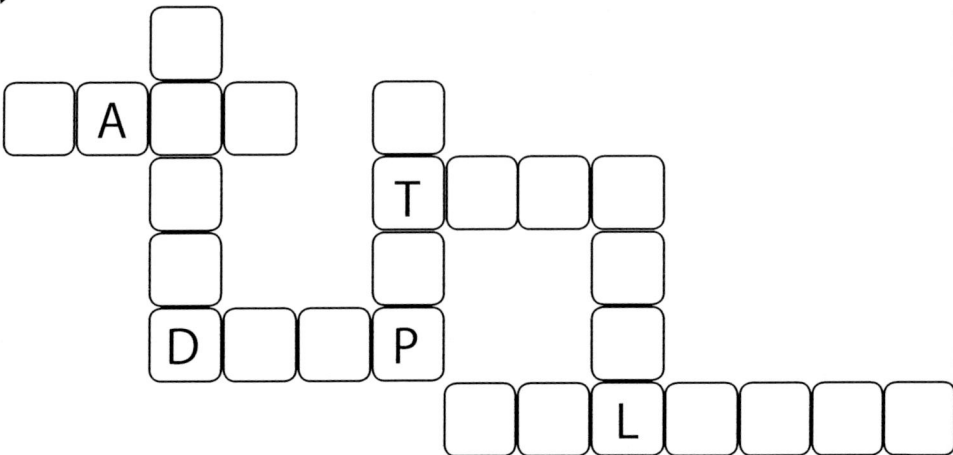

A

T

D P

L

• **Which** list word is not in the puzzle?

_____

Testing Record

List

found
sky
wash
yesterday
woke
clock
coat
suddenly

Extension

skylight skyscraper
washed washing

woken

Interest Words

▶ **Which** list words have three syllables?

_____   _____

• *Write* the three syllables:

____ ____ ____   ____ ____ ____

• **How** many syllables do the other list words have? ☐

2 *Write* a short letter to a friend telling him or her what you did yesterday.

Dear

_ _ _ _ _ _ _ _

Your friend,

_____

3 <u>Connect</u> the words that rhyme and **add** another one:

woke	sock	_____
clock	boat	_____
found	broke	_____
sky	round	_____
coat	cry	_____

4 ▶ **Which** list word ends the same as 'fish'?

_____

• Write some more words that end in '**sh**'.

5 ▶ **Circle** the list or extension words you can find:

becoatsoskylightingwashintipsomcloaknpsyesterday

6 ▶ **Choose** a list word to put in each space:

• Shells _____ up on the beach.

• Mum's going to _____ the fish in crumbs.

• Dad bought Mum a new alarm _____.

Testing Record

List	Extension
stand	standard
yet	yes
head	heading headline
doctor	
mud	muddy
animal	
garden	
word	

Interest Words

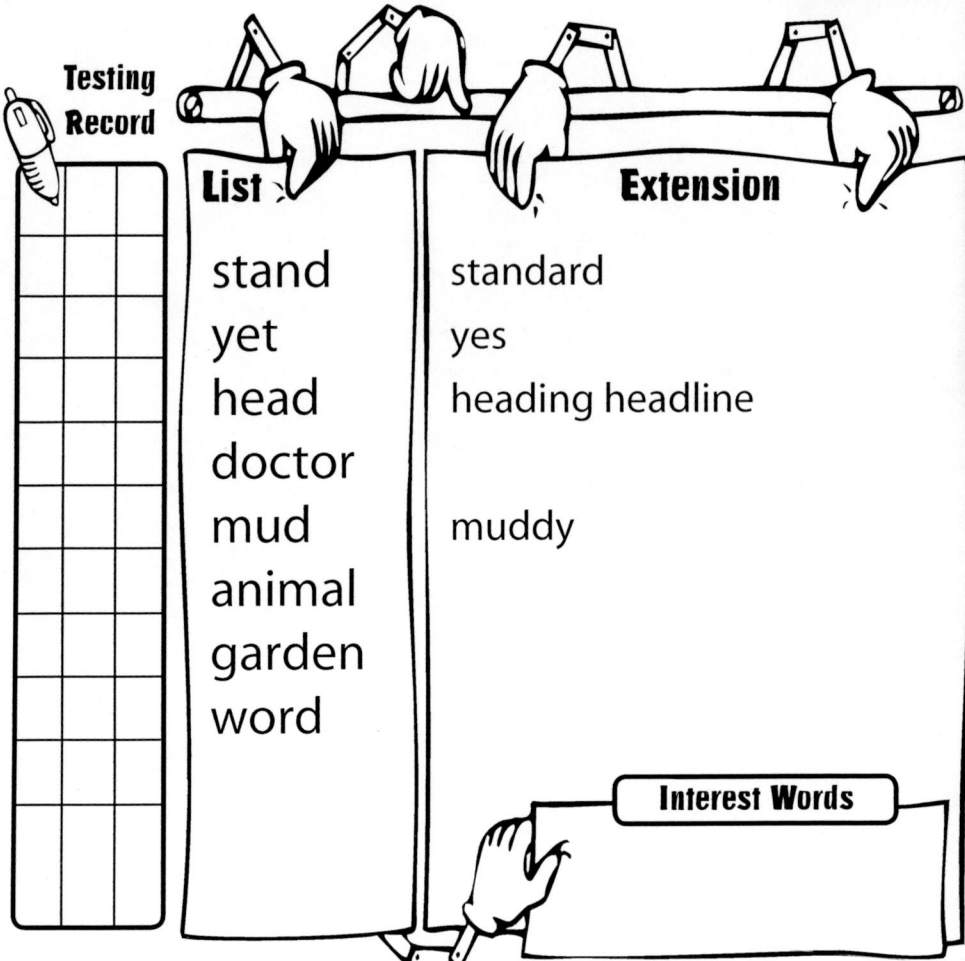

▶ **Complete** word families for the underlined letters in each list word:

st<u>and</u>	y<u>et</u>	h<u>ead</u>
_____	_____	_____
_____	_____	_____
_____	_____	_____
_____	_____	_____
_____	_____	_____

2 <u>**Singular**</u> means one, <u>**plural**</u> means more than one:

• Write the plural of these words:

> Pural means more than one in number.

animal _____

doctor _____

garden _____

word _____

3 An <u>**occupation**</u> is a job that we get paid for:

• **Which** list word is an occupation?

_____

4 Do you like playing in the **mud**?

| **YES** | **NO** |

• If you play in the **mud** you get… | m u d _ _ |

• If you kept playing in the **mud** you would get … | _ _ _ _ _ _ _ |

• If two friends joined you in the **mud** who would be the … | _ _ _ _ _ _ _ _ ? |

Info: When we compare two things we add 'er' . When it is more than two we are comparing we add 'est'. If there is a 'y' at the end of the word we change the 'y' to 'i' before we add 'er' and 'est'.

• **Use 'ier'** and **'iest'** to finish these comparisons:

 Jo is tiny.  Meg is tin_____ than Jo.  Alice is the _____

 happy

 happ_____

 happ_____

 angry

 angr_____

 angr_____

5 **Choose** a list word to fit each gap:

• My pet dog is an _____ .

• I can _____ straight and tall.

• I haven't found my hat _____ .

• It is so very cold and _____ he has shorts on.

• It is so cold that I can't _____ it.

• I don't know how to spell the _____, g_____ .

Testing Record

List

dress
flower
ear
number
slow
second
sister
birthday

Extension

dresser dressy dressing
sunflower flowery
year

slowly

Interest Words

▶ Write the words for the numerals from **0** to **10**:

_____   _____

_____   _____

_____   _____

_____   _____

_____   _____

2 **Which** list word is a part of our body?

_____

• **What** other parts of the body can you name?

 _____   _____

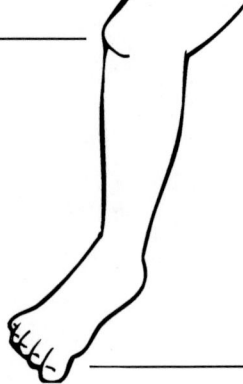

 _____

_____

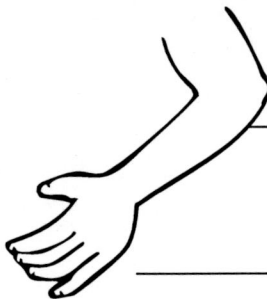 _____

 _____

· ·

3

• **Add 'es'** to dress to make it **plural**:

_____

When a word ends in 'ss' we add 'es' to make it <u>plural</u>.

• **Add 's'** to the other nouns in the list to make them plural.

_____   _____

_____   _____

_____   _____

• **Make** the extension word that rhymes with ears, plural.

_____

4 Put a list word in the gaps. The last one is tricky!

• _____ down, you're going too fast!

• I hear with my _____.

• What _____ is on the card?

• I came _____ in the race.

• I have a new _____ to wear to the party.

• That pink _____ smells very nice.

• Today it is my _____'s _____ _____.

5 Write a sentence using <u>flowery</u> or <u>sunflower</u>:

_____

• Write a sentence using <u>dressy</u> or <u>dressing</u>:

_____

6 Which list words have only one syllable?

© Curriculum Concepts - Spell Now - Book 4

Testing Record

List	Extension
quick	quicker quickest quickly
easy	easier easiest easily
elephant	
can't	
don't	
whole	wholemeal
half	halfway
square	

Interest Words

▶ When we *write* the letter '**q**' we always follow it with a '**u**'
'**qu**' says (**kw**).

• *Write* the '**qu**' word from the list:

_____

• **Read** the words. Can you hear the (**kw**) sound?

• *Write* '**qu**' in front of these letters

_ _ **een**   _ _ **ite**

_ _ **iet**   _ _ **ack**

2 **Which** list word is an animal? _____

• **How** many syllables in this list word? [ ]

• **Which** *two* letters make an '**f**' sound? [__ __]

• **Other** words with this sound in them.

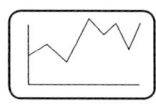

   abc

_____ _____ _____

• **What** little animal can you see in the letters of 'elephant'? [ ]

3 When we add a suffix to a word ending in '**y**' we change the '**y**' to '**i**' then add the suffix:

Add 'er' to easy; easi_ _

Add 'est' to easy; easi_ _ _

A suffix is a group of letters that makes a sound, added to the end of a word. It changes or adds to the meaning of the word slightly.

• *Write* the correct words in the sentences:

This word is (*easy, easier, easiest*) _____ .

List 5 words were (*easy, easier, easiest*) _____ .

List 1 words were the (*easy, easier, easiest*) _____ .

4 **Finish** these well-known phrases:

as quick as _____

as easy as _____

5 **Complete** the sentence:

I don't want _____ an apple, I want

a _____ apple. I am hungry.

6 **Colour** in half of each shape.
Which list word matches one of these shapes?

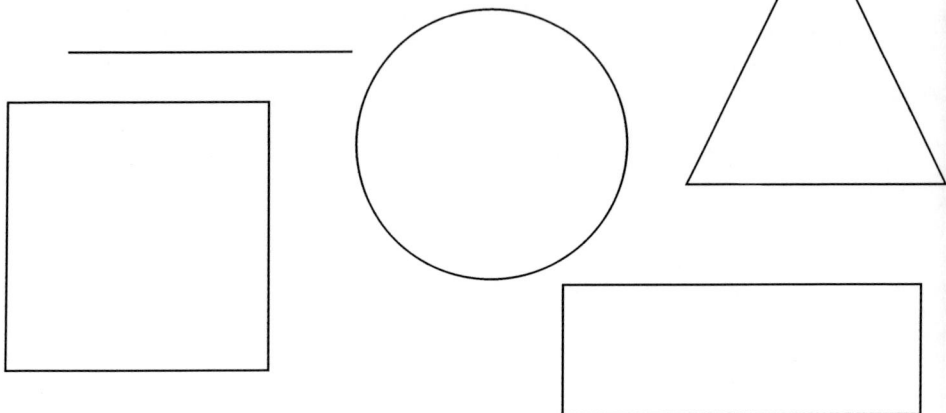

_____

7 **Contraction**

When **two** words are shortened to **one** word it is called a contraction.

can not → can't

· **What** letters are missing?

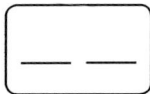

The apostrophe shows that these letters are missing.

don't is short for _____ _____.

· *Write three* other contractions you know.

_____ _____ _____

Testing Record

List

without
until
catch
eye
afraid
something
cone
outside
knew

Extension

undo unlike
caught

eyelid eyelash
unafraid

inside
know

Interest Words

▶ **Which** list words have a silent letter at the end?

_____

_____

_____

• **Which** letter is silent?

• **Which** list word has a silent letter at the beginning?

_____

• **Which** letter is silent?

• **Do** you know another word where this letter is silent?

_____

2 **Which** list word has a prefix?

_____

• **Circle** the prefix.

• *Write* the word with the prefix.

A prefix is a syllable added to the beginning of a word. ('Pre' means before).

un+done = _____

un+do = _____

un+afraid = _____

un+used = _____

3 We use '**a**' and '**an**' before **nouns** (naming words).
When the **noun begins** with a **consonant** we use '**a**'.
When a **noun begins** with a **vowel** we use '**an**'.

• **Put** '**a**' or '**an**' before these words:

___ **ice cream**

___ **arrow**

___ **cone**

___ **banana**

___ **eye**

___ **idea**

4 Label the parts of this face:

_____

_____

_____

_____

_____

5 Write the list words that are compound words:

_____   _____   _____

• **Make** more compound words:

some + _____   =   _____

out + _____   =   _____

_____ + side   =   _____

6 Build these triangles to make list words:

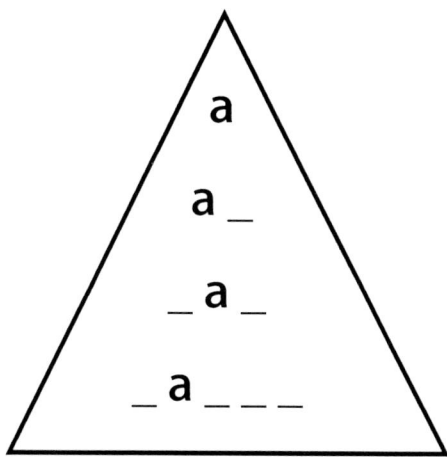

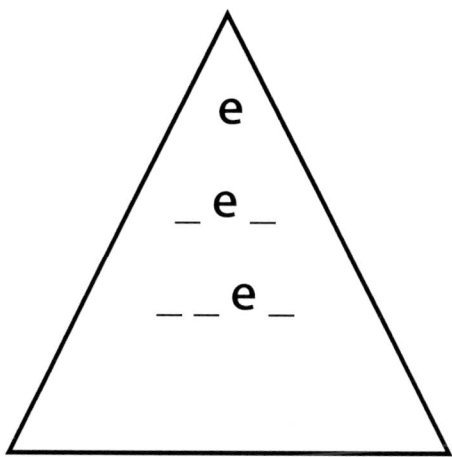

```
        a
       a _
      _ a _
     _ a _ _ _
```

```
        e
       _ e _
      _ _ e _
```

7 Choose the right word:

• I (*know, no*) how to spell all my words.

• That girl is (*new, knew*) here.

• I wish I (*knew, new*) what was in that box.

• (*No, Know*), you can't have an ice cream.

Testing Record

List	Extension
follow	follower following
around	surround
brought	bought
much	
often	
sound	
better	best
great	
asked	

Interest Words

▶ **Which** list words have *two* letters the same together?

_____   _____

• **Which** one of these words means to come along behind?

_____

2 **Brought** is the past tense of **bring**.

I will **bring** my cat to school tomorrow.

I **brought** my cat to school yesterday.

• **Bought** is the past tense of **buy**.

I will **buy** a hat in town.

I **bought** a hat in town yesterday.

• **Complete** the sentence with **bought** or **brought**.

Mum _____ me a new bag.

Tom _____ his toy cars with him.

The boys _____ the frog they caught to show us.

Look what I _____ with my pocket money.

3 **List** all the blended consonants in the list words:

beginning	middle	end

4 ▶ **Put** the list words into alphabetical order.

_____   _____

_____   _____

_____   _____

_____   _____

_____

5 ▶ **'ea'** together **usually** makes the long **'e'** sound as in **beat**.
Write two other words you know with this sound and spelling.

_____   _____

• **What** sound does 'ea' make in the word great?
  It is the odd one out.

Great means   _____

There is another word that sounds the same but is spelt differently - grate.

Grate means   _____

• ⬭Circle the correct word.

• Dad stacked the (_grate, great_) with wood.

• I feel (_great, grate_) today.

• Help me (_grate, great_) the cheese.

Testing Record

List

set
above
rub
across
chase
mine
might
jump
watch

Extension

settle settling settler
about
rubber rubbish

jumps jumped jumping

Interest Words

▶ **Which** list words have a silent 'e' at the end?

_____

_____

_____

• *Write two* rhyming words for each of them:

_____ _____ _____

_____ _____ _____

Sometimes 'e' comes at the end of a word and doesn't make a sound. We will call it <u>silent</u>.

2 Write the consonants in the list words that are side by side:

___ ___   ___ ___ ___   ___ ___ ___

• Write *two* other words beginning with '**ch**':

_____

_____

• Write *two* other words ending with '**tch**':

_____

_____

• Write *two* other words with a '**cr**' sound:

_____

• Write *two* other words ending in '**ght**':

_____

The letters a e i o u
are called vowels.
All the other letters are
called <u>consonants</u>
bcdfghjklmnpqrstvwxyz

A <u>possessive pronoun</u> tells us about
<u>owning</u> (eg his, hers, theirs) The word
is used instead of a noun already
mentioned eg 'Where is <u>Jane</u>?'
'Those are <u>her</u> shoes.'

3 Write the list word that is a possessive pronoun:

⌐ ‐ ‐ ‐ ‐ ‐ ‐ ‐ ‐ ‐ ‐ ‐ ‐ ‐ ‐ ⌐
¦ _____ ¦
└ ‐ ‐ ‐ ‐ ‐ ‐ ‐ ‐ ‐ ‐ ‐ ‐ ‐ ‐ ‐ ┘

• Write the word for the phrase:

belonging to them_____

belonging to me _____

belonging to you _____

belonging to us _____

belonging to him _____

belonging to her _____

belonging to it _____

4 Make a word family of *ten* words or more from **set:**

set	_____
_____	_____
_____	_____
_____	_____
_____	_____

• **Make** a word family of *seven* words or more from **rub:**

rub	_____
_____	_____
_____	_____
_____	_____
_____	_____

• **Which** words in the '**set**' family can you add '**ter**' to? *Write* them:

_____	_____
_____	_____
_____	_____
_____	

• **Which** words in the '**rub**' family can you add '**ber**' to? *Write* them:

_____	_____
_____	_____
_____	

• **Read** all the new words.

5 **Complete** the sentence with **jump, jumps, jumped** or **jumping**:

How many _____ can you do?

I can _____ off the chair.

Look at the kangaroo _____ along.

After the rain yesterday, I _____ over the puddles.

Testing Record

List

dam
write
while
road
bone
rush
blow
these
world

Extension

damp dampen
wrote
white whine
roadway roadside

Interest Words

Put circles around the list words:

e	l	t	h	e	s	e
h	e	d	v	e	w	e
b	s	n	a	o	h	t
l	c	u	l	m	i	i
o	o	c	r	k	l	r
w	e	n	o	b	e	w

• **Which** list words are missing?

• **What** do the letters that are left spell?

_____

2 Finish the explanation: An **abbreviation** is . . .

• **What** are these letters abbreviations for?

Rd _____   Pl _____

St _____   Mr _____

Ave _____

3 Say this word, '**write**'.

Write a **homonym** or **homophone** for write: _____

• Write the correct words in the sentence:

I will _____ the _____ word.

Here is another word that is said the same but spelt differently 'wright'.

• **Look up** this '**wright**' in the dictionary.

• **What** does it mean?

_____

_____

• **Finish** the words: ship_____   play_____

• Write a homonym for road: _____

• Write the correct words in the sentences:

I _____ down the _____ .

4 Fill in the gaps with the different tenses:

Past	Present	Present
_____	**rush**	**is** _____
_____	**blow**	**is** _____
_____	**write**	**is** _____

Write your own example.

_____   _____   _____

5 (Circle) the four errors in this sentence:

Whial there is time, we will dog up the boans from the damm.

• *Rewrite* the sentence without any errors.

_____

6 **Choose** the correct words from the box to finish the sentences.

Take _____ bone.

_____ are cool hats.

that   those   them
this   these

Give the cakes to _____ hungry children.

They will enjoy _____.

Testing Record

List

beg
admit
cross
sea
face
corner
shut
cake
turn

Extension

began

admission admitted admire

crossword crossroad

seaside seagull

Interest Words

▷ **Say** this sound 'or'.

• Write some '**or**' words:

_____ _____

_____ _____

_____ _____

_____ _____

• Write '**or**' '**ur**' '**er**' '**ar**' '**ir**'
in the gaps:

sist ___   f ___ st

c ___ ner   c ___ t

t ___ n

2 Write the list words with a letter 'c' in them:

• **Which** 'c' word sounds different from the others?

• Write the 'c' plus the following letter in each word:

• In **which** word does the 'c' sound like an 's'?

3 _Synonyms_ are words that mean the same.

• Write a synonym for these words:

beg _____   admit _____   shut _____

cross_____

You may use a dictionary or thesaurus.

4 **Make** a family of four words from **turn**:

_____   _____

_____   _____

•**Make** a family of four words from **cake**:

_____   _____

_____   _____

5 Unjumble these sentences:

of the corner Who face the drew this cake? on

_____

the we see door can't the Shut sea. so

_____

food. admit had for that to your beg Don't you

_____

6 **What** does this sound say?

'ea' says [_____]

• **What** other letters make the same sound?

• **Choose** the correct digraph for these words:

p __ ce   rec___ve   s ____

t ____   h ___ t   p __ ce

s ____   t ____

> A digraph is two or three letters which make one sound which is different to the sounds those letters usually make.
> eg 'ie' as in piece
> 'ey' as in money
> 'ph' as in phone

7 Circle the list words:

shutsecafaceadmcrossacornerbocakeadmit

Testing Record

List	Extension
game	gape gave gate
enjoy	enjoyable
drive	driven drove
talk	talkative
asleep	
bill	
queen	
ahead	
money	

Interest Words

▶ **From** the list *write* the words with long vowel sounds:

_____   _____

_____   _____

• **Which** *two* words have vowel sounds that are the same?

_____   _____

• *Write* the letters that make the vowel sound: ☐

• *Write* five more words that use the same letters to make the same vowel sound:

2 **Complete** this word tree using the list words:

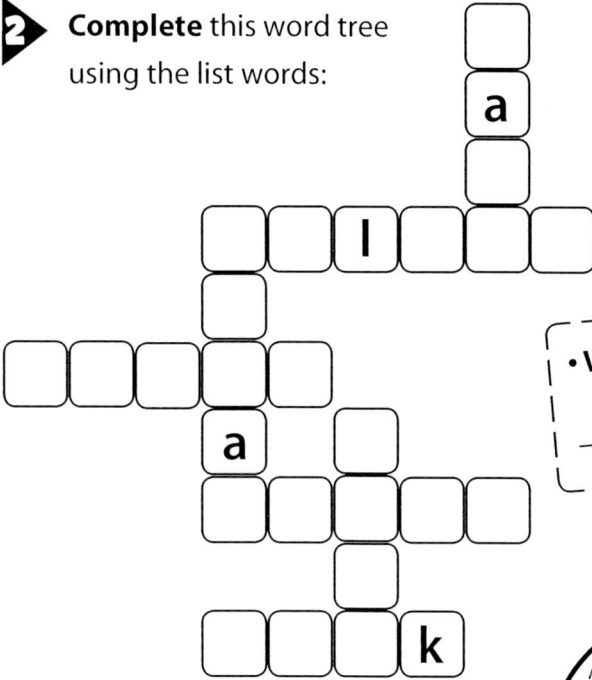

a

l

a

k

┌ ─ ─ ─ ─ ─ ─ ─ ─ ─ ─ ─ ─ ─ ─ ┐
│ • **Which** list word is missing?
│
│ _____
└ ─ ─ ─ ─ ─ ─ ─ ─ ─ ─ ─ ─ ─ ─ ┘

A <u>homograph</u> is a word that is spelt the same but has a different meaning.

3 *Write* the word next to the picture:

_____

_____

_____

_____

4 ▶ **Who** is the queen of the British Commonwealth?

Q _____ E _____

• **Who** is her husband?

P _____ P _____

• **Who** is her eldest son?

_____ _____

• **Who** is his eldest son?

_____ _____

> *Notice that we use capital letters at the beginning of proper nouns.*

5 ▶ **What** sound does the letter '**y**' make in the word:

enjoy ☐ money ☐

6 ▶ **Copy** the dictionary meanings of these list words:

ahead _____

enjoy _____

game _____

Testing Record

List

hand
behave
should
flap
dine
fog
war
bean
mother

Extension

handle handlebar
behaviour
shouldn't
flop flip

Interest Words

▶ **Answer** these questions with list words:

What is thick, wet air? _____

What do we eat that is green or yellow? _____

What is another word for 'eat'? _____

What do we have that has five fingers? _____

2 **Say** this word, **'war'**

Does it **rhyme** with **'tar'**?

YES / NO

• Read these words. (Circle) the ones with a sound like war:

ward

warm

warn

part

warp

wart

smart

• Match the words with the pictures:

wart

warm

warp

ward

warn

Use a dictionary if you need to.

3 Write the names of these vegetables:

Make sure you spell them correctly.

 _____

 _____

 _____

_____

• **Which** list word is the name of a vegetable?

•**Which** word has the same vowel sound as 'bean'? _____

• Write the correct word in the blank:

It has (been, bean) _____ raining so the (beens, beans) _____
(would, should) _____ grow.

4 ▶ Write the 'should' word family:

should

c_____

w_____

5 ▶ An **antonym** is a word that means the opposite.

• Write the list words that are antonyms for these words:

misbehave _____

peace _____

6 ▶ A **compound** word is made up of two little words.

Write a compound word from the list.

_____ = _____ + _____

• **Use** one word from the list to make a compound word.

_____basin _____horn _____time

• Write these compound words:

a + head = _____

a + cross = _____

hair + brush = _____

eye + lid = _____

Testing Record

List

clothes
joy
thought
glad
sleep
fine
aim
jar
father

Extension

joyful
thoughtless
gladly
sleepy slept

aimless

Interest Words

▶ Write a list word in the blanks:

I'll need warm _____ to wear.

I am _____ I bought it as it is a _____ jar.

I _____ I would _____ well after my party.

2 Which *two* list words have similar meanings?

_____ **and** _____

• *Write* the correct one in each space:

When I am happy I am full of _____.

I am _____ I can make you happy.

• *Write* some more 'joy' words:

3 Change '**aim**' to jar by changing *one* letter at a time:

aim

_ _ **r**

f _ _

_ _ _

jar

4 Build these sentences by **adding** the correct endings:

Today it is fine, yesterday was fin____, but I

hope tomorrow will be the fin____ of all.

5 ▶ **Put** the list words into alphabetical order:

_____   _____

_____   _____

_____   _____

_____   _____

_____

6 ▶ **Add** 'ful', 'ous', 'fully' to 'joy':

joy_____

joy_____

joy_____

A suffix is a group
of letters that makes a sound,
added on the end of a word.
It changes or adds to the
meaning of the
word slightly.

• Write some more words with these suffixes
or adding suffixes where needed:

_____ful   _____ous

hope_____   _____fully

hand_____   wonder_____

Testing Record

List

part
hid
through
enter
love
shed
bake
tree
gladly

Extension

partner partnership hidden
hideout
throughout
entertain

Interest Words

▷ Match the list words with the parts of speech:

verb   **tree**

noun   **gladly**

noun   **bake**

adverb   **shed**

*An underline adverb is a word which describes the verb.
An 'adverb' helps tell—when, how, why, where, how much (to what degree)
eg. the boat sank rapidly*

2 **Say** this word, '**love**'.

• Write a rhyming family for 'love'.

love   d _____

a _ ove   gl _____   sh _____

• **Look up** in your dictionary or an encyclopedia to find out what a <u>plover</u> is:

• Draw a picture of one.

3 <u>**Plurals**</u> mean more than one:

• Write the plurals of these words:

part   _____   dart   _____

shed   _____   bed   _____

tree   _____   bee   _____

4 **Which** list word has two syllables?

• Match the list words to the suffixes
to make them two syllable words:

• Write the new words:

part   ly

hid   ner

love   ry

bake   den

5 **Say** this word, 'through'
Say this word, 'threw'

These words are homophones
because they sound the same
but have different spelling.

•Write the correct word in the gaps:

I (*through, threw*) _____ the ball over the

fence, then I crawled (*through, threw*) _____

the fence to get it.

6 **Find** the smaller words inside these words:

shed

part

through

hid

Testing Record

List

tar
feed
art
ill
nose
another
dip
street

Extension

target tart
food fed
artist artwork

Interest Words

▶ **1** **Find** *five* small words in '**another**':

....

▶ **2** *Write* all the consonants in the list words in **alphabetical** order:

3 Match the words with the same vowel sounds:

tar	street
feed	dip
ill	cone
nose	art

• Write another 'ar' word:
_____

• Write another 'ee' word:
_____

• Write another 'i' word:
_____

• Write another 'o_e' word:
_____

4 **Say** this word, 'ill'

• The 'i' sound is **short/long**
(cross one out)

• **Why** does 'Jill' have a capital letter?

It is a _____ **noun.**

• **Build** an 'ill' word family:

_ill

_____ _____ _____ _____

qu____

_____ _____ _____ _____

• **Read** this word, 'nil'. It is an unusual word because it only has one 'l'.

• Write it in this sentence and read it aloud.

The soccer score was three _____ .

5 An **adjective** is a word that describes a noun.

• Write an adjective for these nouns:

_____ tar   _____ street

_____ nose

6 Unjumble these list words:

pdi   _____   oetnrah   _____

tra   _____   edfe   _____

7 Circle the list words:

I'mfeedworkingartveryillhardnoseattarlearningstreettoanotherspelldip

• **Take** the first letter of each list word in the order they appear above. What two words can you make?

__ __ __ __ __   __ __ __

• **What** do the words between the list words say?

Testing Record

List

baby
odd
place
dark
jet
hit
okay
dive

Extension

babysit babysitter
oddment
placement
dart darn

Interest Words

Write the list words in the correct columns:

3 letters   **4 letters**   **5 letters**

1 syllable

_____   _____

_____   _____

_____   _____

_____

2 syllables

_____   _____

0 vowel   # 2 vowels

_____   _____

_____   _____

_____   _____

_____   _____

Is 'y' a vowel?
Yes
No
Sometimes

. . . .

> **Put** these prefixes in front of list words:

un _____

mis _____

re _____

• To lose means to

mis_____.

• To put back in place means to...

_____

3 Write the word under the picture (first one starts with a list word):

_____   _____   _____   _____   _____

• A very young person is a _____

• A grown-up is an _____

• You are a _____

4 Say this word, 'place'

What sound does the 'c' make? [   ]

What letter comes after the 'c'? [   ]

5 Write three sentences using as many list words as you can:

_____

_____

_____

_____

_____

_____

• **Complete** this 'ace' word family.

ace

r_____

pl _____

br _____

f_____

gr _____

l_____

p _____

m_____

Testing Record

List	Extension
before	beforehand
inside	outside underside
band	bandage bandit
farm	farmer
orange	
cousin	
also fade	
ago	

Interest Words

▶ **Which** list words have silent 'e' letters?

• **Where** does that silent 'e' come in the word? At the _____.

• *Write* another two words that have a silent 'e':

_____   _____

in	us	ge	_____
or	si	re	_____
be	an	in	_____
co	fo	de	_____ inside

3 **Which** list word is a fruit? [   ]

• *Write* the names of these fruit.

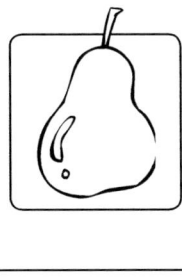

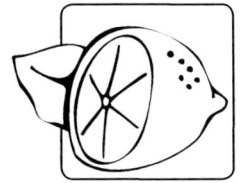

_____

_____   _____

4 **What** letter is in all these words?

ago   band   also   farm   fade   [ ]

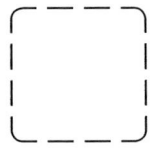

• **Say** the words.

• Does the letter sound the same in any two words?   **Yes / No.**

5 ▶ **Build** this triangular word:

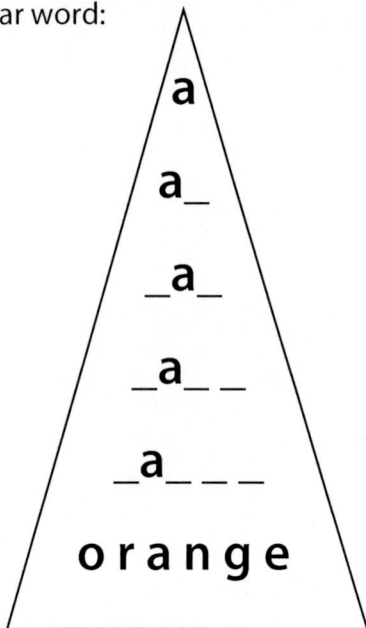

```
        a
        a _
      _ a _
      _ a _ _
    _ a _ _ _
    o r a n g e
```

6 ▶ *Write* the words under the correct picture:

uncle

brother

mother   grandmother

sister

father   aunt   grandfather   cousin

Testing Record

List

cage
miss
save
left
joke
during
between
ball
town

Extension

cagey
misspell
savour savoury
cleft deft

Interest Words

▶ **Say** these words, 'cage', 'joke'

• **Which** letters sound the same? ☐ and ☐

• **Say** these words:

giant   go
gentle
gun   gate

▶ • **What** letters make the 'g' sound like a 'j'?

☐ and ☐

2 Write the list word that rhymes with each of these words, and add another:

clown _____ _____

tall _____ _____

hiss _____ _____

brave _____ _____

3 Find the list words:

b	n	a	t	b	c	d	d	e
e	w	b	f	e	f	u	g	g
t	o	a	e	h	r	a	i	j
w	t	l	l	i	c	k	l	m
e	n	l	n	j	o	k	e	o
e	p	g	s	s	i	m	q	r
n	e	v	a	s	s	t	u	v

• Write out the other letters:

4 Which list words have a silent 'e' at the end?

_____ _____ _____

• Write the plurals of those nouns:

_____ _____

5 ▶ **Add** the other tenses to these list words:

Past	Present	Future
left	_____	_____ _____
_____	*miss*	_____ _____
_____	_____	will save

. . . .

6 ▶ Unjumble this word:

nebetew _____

• Write other two syllable words beginning with '**be**'.

be _____   be _____

be _____   be _____

be _____   be _____

. . . .

7 ▶ **Use** a list word to fill each space:

_____ the interval, _____ the

first and second half of play, I _____

the _____ hall.

Testing Record

List

behind
none
cross
form
girl
enough
dinner
age
dance

Extension

beneath below nonetheless
crossover
formal format

Interest Words

▶ Write the pronouns for these nouns:

The girl ate her dinner while _____ read a book.

The boy rode the big horse while _____ still felt brave.

Max chewed his bone as_____ still had meat on it.

> A pronoun is a word used instead of a noun. eg him, her, they, she, we and he.

2▶ **Say** this word, **'enough'**.

• *Write* the letters **'ough'** sounds like:

• *Write* another **'ough'** word that rhymes with enough?

3▶ *Write* the *two* list words containing the letter **'c'**:

• **Which** **'c'** sounds like an **'s'**? _____

• **What** letter comes after the **'c'**? _____

• *Write* another word that ends in **'ce'**: _____

•*Write* *three* more words beginning with **'cr'**:

cr_____   cr_____   cr_____

4▶ *Write* the **'be'** word in the correct place:

Use 'before'
'behind'
'between'

5 Which list word means 'not one' or 'no one'?

• Write it in a sentence:

_____

_____

6 Unjumble these sentences:

the to dinner. None girls of went the

_____

age be thirteen. needed Their to

_____

to They put form. the on had truth the

_____

_____

7 Complete the phrases using list words:

in fine _____   _____ the times

have had _____   _____-country

_____ the less   come of _____

_____patch   _____bar   _____ other than

Testing Record

List

fact
favour
happy
flash
fell
night
oven
cave
bird

Extension

factor factory
favourite favourable
happier happiest
flashy

Interest Words

▶ A **_mnemonic_** (silent first 'm') helps us to learn or remember something. We can use a mnemonic to help us remember how to spell a word by making a sentence using the letters of the word as first letters in words of a sentence. A mnemonic for **_FACT_** might be **_Fat Ants Can Talk_**.

• **Make** up your own mnemonic for **bird**, **night**, and **favour**:

B_____ I_____ R_____ D_____

N_____ I_____ G_____ H_____ T_____

F____ A_____ V_____ O_____ U_____ R_____

2 *Four* words in the list begin with the letter '**f**':

•*Write* them in alphabetical order:

f_____   f_____   f_____   f_____

•In your **dictionary** find a word beginning with '**fo**', one beginning with '**fi**' and one beginning with '**fr**'. Now put all the '**f**' words in **alphabetical** order:

f_____   f_____   f_____

f_____   f_____   f_____

f_____

3 *We put '**a**' before a noun beginning with a consonant.*
*We put '**an**' before a noun beginning with a vowel.*

• *Write* the nouns from your list:
• (Circle) the correct '**a**' or '**an**' before each noun.

an/a _____

an/a _____   an/a _____

an/a _____   an/a _____

an/a _____   an/a _____

• *Write* three more nouns that begin with a vowel.

• *Write* '**an**' in the box before each one:

☐ _____   ☐ _____   ☐ _____

4 ▶ Fill in the gaps:

A _____ is an animal with feathers.

A _____ is an animal that lives in water.

A _____ is an animal that gives birth to live young.

An _____ is an animal with six legs.

5 ▶ **Choose** the correct word to fill the gap:

We cook in an (*open, oven*) _____.

We smile when we are (*happy, nappy*) _____.

It is fun to explore a (*cape, cave*) _____.

• *Write* these words in sentences
of your own:

oven happy cave

_____

_____

_____

6 ▶ **'Night'** has some silent letters.

• **Make** a word family for night:

night

_____ _____

f_____ _____ _____

_____ _____ _____

© Curriculum Concepts - Spell Now - Book 4

My Test Results

LIST	PRE-TEST Nº Correct	Words to learn	POST-TEST Nº Correct	Words I **still** need to learn
1				
2				
3				
4				
5				
6				
7				
8				
9				
10				

My Test Results

LIST	PRE-TEST N° Correct	Words to learn	POST-TEST N° Correct	Words I **still** need to learn
11				
12				
13				
14				
15				
16				
17				
18				
19				
20				

My Test Results

LIST	PRE-TEST Nº Correct	Words to learn	POST-TEST Nº Correct	Words I **still** need to learn
21				
22				
23				
24				
25				

Review test after post test

Words to learn [ ]

Words that still catch me out.

_____

_____

_____

_____

_____

_____

_____

Test 1
Words correct [ ]

Review test 2

Words to learn [ ]

Words I still need to work on.

_____

_____

_____

_____

_____

_____

_____

Test 2
Words correct [ ]